SOME MAJOR EVENTS IN WORLD WAR II

THE EUROPEAN THEATER

1939 SEPTEMBER—Germany invades Poland; Great Britain, France, Australia, & New Zealand declare war on Germany; Battle of the Atlantic begins. NOVEMBER—Russia invades Finland.

1940 APRIL—Germany invades Denmark & Norway. MAY—Germany invades Belgium, Luxembourg, & The Netherlands; British forces retreat to Dunkirk and escape to England. JUNE—Italy declares war on Britain & France; France surrenders to Germany. JULY—Battle of Britain begins. SEPTEMBER—Italy invades Egypt; Germany, Italy, & Japan form the Axis countries. OCTOBER—Italy invades Greece. NOVEMBER—Battle of Britain over. DECEMBER—Britain attacks Italy in North Africa.

1941 JANUARY—Allies take Tobruk. FEBRUARY—Rommel arrives at Tripoli. APRIL—Germany invades Greece & Yugoslavia. JUNE—Allies are in Syria; Germany invades Russia. JULY—Russia joins Allies. AUGUST—Germans capture Kiev. OCTOBER—Germany reaches Moscow. DECEMBER—Germans retreat from Moscow; Japan attacks Pearl Harbor; United States enters war against Axis nations.

1942 MAY—first British bomber attack on Cologne. JUNE—Germans take Tobruk. SEPTEMBER—Battle of Stalingrad begins. OCTOBER—Battle of El Alamein begins. NOVEMBER—Allies recapture Tobruk; Russians counterattack at Stalingrad.

1943 JANUARY—Allies take Tripoli. FEBRUARY—German troops at Stalingrad surrender. APRIL—revolt of Warsaw Ghetto Jews begins. MAY—German and Italian resistance in North Africa is over; their troops surrender in Tunisia; Warsaw Ghetto revolt is put down by Germany. JULY—allies invade Sicily; Mussolini put in prison. SEPTEMBER—Allies land in Italy; Italians surrender; Germans occupy Rome; Mussolini rescued by Germany. OCTOBER—Allies capture Naples; Italy declares war on Germany. NOVEMBER—Russians recapture Kiev.

1944 JANUARY—Allies land at Anzio. JUNE—Rome falls to Allies; Allies land in Normandy (D-Day). JULY—assassination attempt on Hitler fails. AUGUST—Allies land in southern France. SEPTEMBER—Brussels freed. OCTOBER—Athens liberated. DECEMBER—Battle of the Bulge.

1945 JANUARY—Russians free Warsaw. FEBRUARY—Dresden bombed. APRIL—Americans take Belsen and Buchenwald concentration camps; Russians free Vienna; Russians take over Berlin; Mussolini killed; Hitler commits suicide. MAY—Germany surrenders; Goering captured.

THE PACIFIC THEATER

1940 SEPTEMBER—Japan joins Axis nations Germany & Italy.

1941 APRIL—Russia & Japan sign neutrality pact. DECEMBER—Japanese launch attacks against Pearl Harbor, Hong Kong, the Philippines, & Malaya; United States and Allied nations declare war on Japan; China declares war on Japan, Germany, & Italy; Japan takes over Guam, Wake Island, & Hong Kong; Japan attacks Burma.

1942 JANUARY—Japan takes over Manila; Japan invades Dutch East Indies. FEBRUARY—Japan takes over Singapore; Battle of the Java Sea. APRIL—Japanese overrun Bataan. MAY—Japan takes Mandalay; Allied forces in Philippines surrender to Japan; Japan takes Corregidor; Battle of the Coral Sea. JUNE—Battle of Midway; Japan occupies Aleutian Islands. AUGUST—United States invades Guadalcanal in the Solomon Islands.

1943 FEBRUARY—Guadalcanal taken by U.S. Marines. MARCH—Japanese begin to retreat in China. APRIL—Yamamoto shot down by U.S. Air Force. MAY—U.S. troops take Aleutian Islands back from Japan. JUNE—Allied troops land in New Guinea. NOVEMBER—U.S. Marines invade Bougainville & Tarawa.

1944 FEBRUARY—Truk liberated. JUNE—Saipan attacked by United States. JULY—battle for Guam begins. OCTOBER—U.S. troops invade Philippines; Battle of Leyte Gulf won by Allies.

1945 JANUARY—Luzon taken; Burma Road won back. MARCH—Iwo Jima freed. APRIL—Okinawa attacked by U.S. troops; President Franklin Roosevelt dies; Harry S. Truman becomes president. JUNE—United States takes Okinawa. AUGUST—atomic bomb dropped on Hiroshima; Russia declares war on Japan; atomic bomb dropped on Nagasaki. SEPTEMBER—Japan surrenders.

WORLD AT WAR
Battle of Midway

WORLD AT WAR

Battle of Midway

By G.C. Skipper

 CHILDRENS PRESS, CHICAGO

Pearl Harbor (above) was the site of the code room in which the Japanese message about a coming attack was received.

FRONTISPIECE:
Japanese Zeros and planes from the United States aircraft carrier *Yorktown* (at right) at the beginning of the Battle of Midway.

Library of Congress Cataloging in Publication Data

Skipper, G.C.
  The Battle of Midway.

  (His World at war)
  SUMMARY: Details the June 1942 battle between the Japanese and the Americans which decided the control of the Pacific.
  1. Midway, Battle of, 1942—Juvenile literature.
[1. Midway, Battle of, 1942. 2. World War, 1939-1945—Pacific Ocean] I. Title. II. Series.
D774.M5S56   940.54'26   80-17495
ISBN 0-516-04782-5

PICTURE CREDITS:
OFFICIAL U.S. NAVY PHOTOGRAPH: Cover, pag
4, 6, 8, 9, 11, 13, 14, 15, 19, 21, 23, 24, 27,
(bottom), 33, 37, 39, 41, 43, 45, 46
NATIONAL ARCHIVES: pages 29 (top) and
U.S. AIR FORCE PHOTO: page 30
LEN MEENTS (map): page 17

COVER PHOTO:
Devastator Torpedo Bombers on board t
carrier U.S.S. *Enterprise* before taking off
the Battle of Midway. Only four of thes
planes returned.

"Get somebody in here quick!" shouted the corporal.

He sat at a desk in a huge room that was hidden behind mammoth metal doors. Some mornings the corporal felt as if he worked inside a bank vault, but today he had been too busy to even think about it. He hadn't even thought about the armed guards outside the building. Or the wire fences that kept them all locked behind a solid barrier of secrecy and security.

The corporal reread the message. Maybe he had made a mistake. Maybe he had goofed up somewhere. But as he double checked it, he knew no mistake had been made.

He was part of the Combat Intelligence Unit. It was his job to intercept and decipher Japanese coded messages. Right this minute, as he looked down at the piece of paper in his hand, he wanted to be far away from the Pacific. He wanted to be far away from the war. A shiver ran through his body.

"Did you hear me?" he shouted again. "Get an officer in here! Quick!"

Only a few months earlier, Japan had attacked the American Pacific fleet at Pearl Harbor (above).

The other members of the Intelligence Unit looked up from their desks. For a moment they stared at the corporal.

"It sounds serious," someone commented. He lifted the telephone receiver on his desk.

It was early summer 1942. The United States was locked in furious battle with Japan. When the Japanese had bombed Pearl Harbor it had stunned Americans. The American retaliation was severe and violent. Suddenly World War II had spread from the chaotic, howling battlefronts of Europe to the Pacific.

The "Purple Machine" used by the navy to decode Japanese messages at the beginning of World War II.

Deciphering the Japanese code had taken hundreds of tedious hours. And the job still wasn't done. Only part of the code had been broken. It was the part that still wasn't unscrambled that upset the corporal.

The Japanese were about to attack again—a major attack. That much he understood. What he could not figure out, however, was where.

"What's going on?" The corporal jumped when the officer spoke. While the corporal had been rechecking the message, the officer had entered and crossed the room.

"Look at this, sir," said the corporal, handing over the sheet of paper. The officer read the message quietly and then let out a low whistle.

"Where are they going to hit?" the officer asked.

"That's the problem, sir. All I can make out of the target is the code name 'AF.' Whatever that means."

"You're saying 'AF' could mean anything—Hawaii, Midway, or Coney Island?"

"Yes sir."

The officer reread the message. "We can be pretty sure it's not Coney Island," he said, keeping a straight face. "Washington has been expecting the enemy to hit Oahu. That could be it."

"Do you really think they'd try it again in Hawaii?" asked the corporal.

"I don't. I said that's what Washington thinks. I think 'AF' means Midway. There's one way to find out," said the officer.

The airfield on Easter Island in the Midway Atoll can be seen in the foreground. Sand Island, also part of Midway, is in the background.

"How, sir?"

"There's a distillation plant on Midway. It converts salt water to drinking water. What I want you to do is this: Get word to Midway that they are to radio a message saying the plant is on the blink. I want that message sent in the open so the Japanese will be sure to intercept it. Is that clear?"

"Yes sir," said the corporal.

"We'll know soon enough what 'AF' is," the officer said.

"Sir. If Midway is the target, and if the Japanese take it, they could control the entire Pacific."

"Now you've got it," replied the officer. "Get busy. Let's nail down that target. We haven't much time."

The intelligence unit went to work. Midway radioed the fake message in the open, as ordered. Within two days the intelligence unit learned what it wanted to know. It intercepted a coded message intended for Tokyo. The message warned that 'AF' was short of water.

"That's it," the officer told the corporal. "They're going to attack Midway. I think it's time Uncle Sam organized a little welcoming party."

On June 4, 1942, the Japanese fleet was steaming toward Midway, quietly pushing through dense fog. A Japanese officer, Nagumo, guided four mighty aircraft carriers out across the Pacific. They were the *Akagi*, the *Hiryu*, the *Kaga*, and the *Soryu*.

Vice Admiral Nagumo (above) was in charge of the Japanese attack on Midway.

Nagumo stared through the foggy, early morning. He was worried. The weather should have been clear. Now, with this fog, it was hard to spot enemy aircraft. However, Nagumo knew the fog would help hide the Japanese fleet.

This was extremely important. The entire trip had been made in utmost secrecy and it was urgent that no one discover them. The fog would provide a protective blanket. Nagumo listened to the soft lapping of the waves. Then he turned his mind to the steady, reliable throb of the engines.

A Japanese plane departs from the deck of a carrier.

Soon, Nagumo thought, we will hit them. When we attack Midway, the United States fleet will still be in Hawaii. He smiled to himself.

But Nagumo's smile would have disappeared had he known the truth. What he didn't know was that exactly one day after he set sail with the powerful Japanese fleet, Rear Admiral Raymond A. Spruance of the United States Navy also set sail. He left Pearl Harbor aboard the aircraft carrier *Enterprise*. With him were the carrier *Hornet*, six cruisers, and eleven destroyers.

Rear Admiral Raymond A. Spruance (above) was in charge of the American defense of Midway Atoll.

Two days later, another American commander, Rear Admiral F.J. Fletcher, followed Spruance. Fletcher was aboard the carrier *Yorktown*. With him were two cruisers and six destroyers.

The stage was set for one of the most important battles of World War II—the Battle of Midway.

The Japanese fleet chugged on silently through the night and into the quiet, cool hours of early morning. It was June 4, 1942. That morning was different from the others. Nagumo could feel the excitement that swept among the crew aboard his ship. As he looked out across the water at the other ships, he knew the same excitement was felt there, too.

It was a familiar feeling—the excitement of approaching battle.

Nagumo read his gauges again. The fleet was nearing its target—Midway. "Now it will begin," Nagumo said quietly.

Word spread rapidly from ship to ship. There was suddenly a roar of engines and noise. The

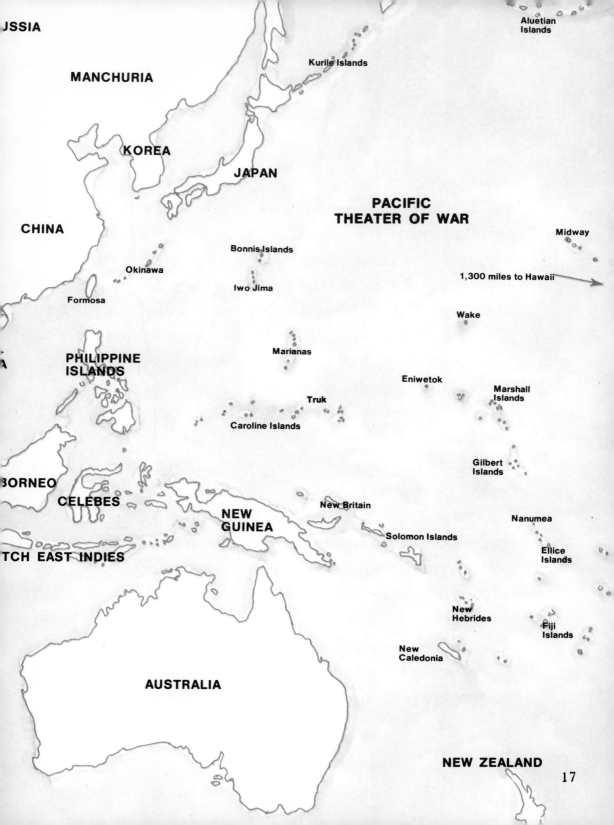

RUSSIA

MANCHURIA

KURILE Islands

Aluetian
Islands

KOREA

JAPAN

PACIFIC
THEATER OF WAR

CHINA

Midway

Bonnis Islands

Okinawa

1,300 miles to Hawaii

Iwo Jima

Formosa

Wake

PHILIPPINE
ISLANDS

Marianas

Eniwetok

Truk

Marshall
Islands

Caroline Islands

BORNEO

Gilbert
Islands

CELEBES

New Britain

Nanumea

NEW
GUINEA

Solomon Islands

Ellice
Islands

TCH EAST INDIES

New
Hebrides

Fiji
Islands

New
Caledonia

AUSTRALIA

NEW ZEALAND

17

shrill yelp of men's voices cut skyward from the decks. Zeros and dive-bombers rolled into position, ready for takeoff.

Suddenly the signal came. The Japanese launched nine Zeros and eighteen dive-bombers from one ship. Within fifteen minutes all four Japanese carriers had cleared their decks. The first aircraft were headed toward Midway.

"Get the reconnaissance planes up!" came the order. "They are to fan out to the east and southeast!"

Five reconnaissance planes roared down the decks. They lifted off the ships and into the sky. The sixth plane lumbered into position. With propellers revved up, it bumped down the deck, gaining speed. Suddenly the plane screeched, fishtailed, and jarred to a halt.

"Catapult trouble!" shouted a Japanese crewman. "Get it back for relaunch!"

The reconnaissance plane was pulled back to the starting position. The propellers whirled again.

Japanese aircraft warm up on the flight deck of the *Hiryu* before the attack on Midway.

The aircraft bounced rapidly down the deck. This time the catapult worked. The plane cleared the deck and climbed slowly into the sky.

Word of the delay reached Nagumo. "How much time did we lose?" he asked.

"Thirty minutes," came the reply. "It is good that the American fleet is still in Hawaii," said Nagumo. "That delay could have been costly."

The reconnaissance planes had one mission—to look for American carriers. Had the Japanese plane not suffered the thirty-minute delay, it would surely have spotted the American fleet. The Midway battle would have changed direction.

As it happened, however, Nagumo was certain the United States ships were many miles away. He turned his attention to the next job—readying thirty-six more planes aboard the *Akagi* and the *Kaga*.

"Are the planes prepared?" Nagumo finally asked.

"Yes sir."

"Get them into the air," said the commander.

Soon the noise of the aircraft engines disappeared and the ships once more cut silently through the waves. Nagumo sighed. The attack planes were off. Things were going very well. Very well indeed.

On Midway, an American pilot—Lieutenant Howard Ady—gulped down the last of his hot

This reconnaissance plane flying over the Pacific Ocean is much like the one flown by Lieutenant Howard Ady as he searched for the Japanese fleet.

coffee. He jogged out to the Catalina search plane waiting for him on the runway. It was early morning, but he was wide awake.

Ady knew the Japanese were going to hit. The alert had come earlier and it had rattled Ady's nerves. It was his job to take the Catalina up and scout the ocean in search of enemy ships. As he jogged toward his plane, Ady felt the pressure of his responsibility.

"Get enough sleep, Lieutenant?" one of the aircraft mechanics called. Ady grinned and waved his hand. He crawled into the cockpit, feeling at home in front of the dials and gauges. He taxied down the runway.

The Catalina picked up speed. Slowly, gracefully, it lifted into the early-morning sky. Ady kept the plane hidden in the clouds. For a while, he flew in safety—at least as much safety as any man could have in this war.

When it was time, Ady lowered his altitude. He dipped down through the cloud bank, sneaking a peep at the ocean below.

As he broke into the clearing, he looked down. He was stunned! Below him stretched the largest mass of ships he'd ever seen! It was incredible! He radioed, "Enemy carriers," and quickly pulled his plane back up into the safety of the clouds. For a moment he waited. Then he breathed a sigh of relief. The Japanese had not seen him.

Carefully he piloted the aircraft through the clouds. Then he swept around in a circle,

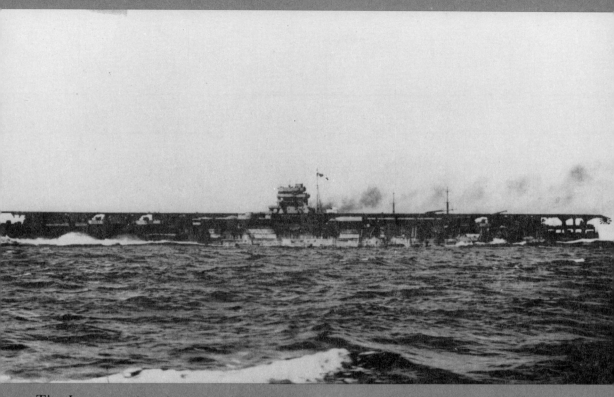

The Japanese aircraft carrier *Hiryu* (above) was one of those spotted by Ady.

gradually descending. He came up low behind the ships. Two carriers! Several more in the formation were battleships. Ady didn't take time to study them too closely. He looked at his wristwatch. The time was 5:25 A.M.

Twenty-five minutes after Ady spotted the enemy fleet, the radar screens on Midway showed

These navy Avenger torpedo planes are heading north from Midway to intercept the Japanese Zeros.

blips. They were the first swarm of Japanese planes that had been launched from the ships. Suddenly the two islands became a bedlam of noise. Sirens screamed warnings, harshly, loudly, repeatedly. Men ran in all directions. Some ran toward planes waiting on runways. Within minutes, American aircraft roared down the runways and took off. Six navy Avenger torpedo planes lifted off from Midway. Then four army Marauders armed with torpedoes climbed upward to meet the enemy. All ten aircraft headed north to intercept the Japanese planes.

Twenty-five Marine fighter pilots grumbled about the obsolete Brewster Buffaloes and Grumman Wildcats they had to fly. But they scampered out to the planes.

"Let's go! Let's go!" shouted a Marine officer. "Get the lead out! This is it! Move it! Move it!"

The planes lifted up and lumbered toward the northwest. For a few minutes the American planes leveled off and roared out to sea. "Whadda ya know," came a Marine's voice over the radio, "these tin cans actually got off the ground."

Before anyone could answer, the Americans suddenly ran head-on into a swarm of Japanese Zeros. The Zeros seemed to come out of nowhere. They were all over the place.

"Look what we found," someone said. But the voice was lost in the sudden rattle of machine-gun fire. The first air battle erupted in a hail of bullets.

"Watch it!" a Marine shouted. There was suddenly a vicious chattering of machine-gun fire. An American plane fell in an ugly swirl of fire downward and into the ocean. The Japanese

Zeros were too much for the lumbering American planes. The Zeros outnumbered the Marines. Fifteen United States aircraft plummeted, trailing smoke, to the ground. The Zeros swatted away the American interceptors like flies and continued toward Midway.

"That was not difficult," a Japanese pilot said. He looked down from his cockpit. Below him was the target—Midway. An order was barked over a radio. The dive-bombers shrilled downward in a screaming attack. American anti-aircraft guns cracked and thudded all around the Japanese planes. But the dive-bombers kept coming.

For twenty minutes the Japanese planes screamed down and unleashed their deadly bombs. Suddenly, the Zeros pulled up and headed back out to sea. Beneath them, Midway was a roaring stretch of flames whipped by the wind. Fires burned everywhere. Black smoke billowed high into the morning sky.

The Japanese pilot looked down. He realized with a shock that the bombing had not crippled

After the Japanese attack, Midway became a roaring stretch of flame and smoke, whipped by the wind.

the Americans. Through the fire and smoke below, he could see United States planes still taking off from runways. Incredible! the Japanese pilot thought. At 7 A.M., as he scampered up and away from the target, Japanese Lieutenant Tomonaga radioed, "There is need for a second attack."

By this time, however, the American planes that had taken off from Midway had spotted the Japanese carriers. Four Marauders and six Avengers bore down on the fleet. Zeros, left behind to guard the fleet, swarmed up to meet the Americans. Three American planes were blasted out of the air.

"Why you dirty—" The American's voice was lost as he aimed his plane down toward the ships. He swept in closer to unload his bombs. Suddenly anti-aircraft fire blasted upward from the ships. The American pilot was hit. His plane went into the ocean. As the air fight raged, another American plane was shot down by anti-aircraft guns.

Three American pilots managed to get through the hail of bullets. The trio dived down toward the *Akagi*.

"Get that ship!" one of the pilots shouted. All three planes launched their torpedoes.

On board the ship, the Japanese were wild with panic. It seemed as if the three American planes

Above: A damaged American bomber on Midway after the attack.

Below: Damage on Midway after the Japanese attack.

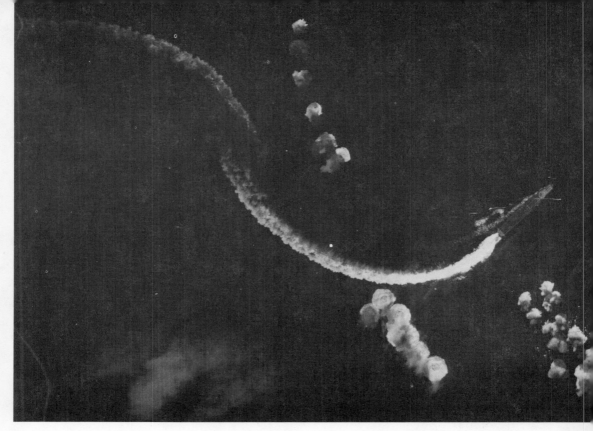

The *Akagi* swerves suddenly in the water to avoid American bombs.

were about to land on the very deck of the *Akagi*. Then the planes swooped up and were gone.

"Torpedo! Torpedo!" came the panic cry aboard ship. "Get out of the way!"

The great ship, in a surprisingly agile motion, swerved suddenly. The crew gazed downward into the water as the torpedo churned harmlessly past the ship. The Americans had missed.

But the near miss didn't make the Japanese feel any better. Things were in a state of confusion.

Anti-aircraft guns were thundering upward at the American planes. Zeros swarmed all over the sky trying to keep the Americans away from the Japanese ships. Torpedoes ploughed through the water, dangerously close.

And in the midst of this bedlam came the request for a second attack on Midway.

"Ready the planes!" shouted a Japanese officer. "Send more planes to Midway! Americans are still taking off!"

Suddenly another message came in. The American fleet had been spotted 240 miles north of Midway! American ships were steaming toward the battle.

"That can't be!" shouted a Japanese commander. "The Americans are still in Hawaii!"

The Japanese commander did not dare to believe the message. Surprised and angry, he shouted: "Identify those ships! I want to know what kind of ships are out there!"

As a crewman scurried away to send the message, suddenly the commander heard a new sound above all the noise. There were planes overhead! American planes!

As he looked up, sixteen American aircraft calmly leveled out and swept toward the ships in a glide-bombing attack.

"Where are the Zeros?" cried the Japanese commander.

As if to answer his question, a squadron of Zeros soared up to meet the Americans. Again machine-gun fire erupted and a solid rain of bullets swept the American planes. Half of the American fighters were dropped. They spiraled, then died in the water. But the others kept coming. Suddenly the Japanese commander realized what they were after—the carrier *Hiryu*.

As the Japanese watched in fear, the bombay doors of the American planes opened. Down came the bombs, tumbling, turning, leveling out in what seemed to be deadly accuracy.

"No!" screamed a Japanese crewman.

But the bombs exploded harmlessly into the sea. The *Hiryu* made it through the attack without a scratch.

These Douglas SBD Dauntless dive-bombers unloaded their bombs on the burning Japanese ship below during the Battle of Midway.

Then, without warning, the attack ended. Just as the Japanese officer breathed a sigh of relief, he was handed another message. The American ships had been identified.

He couldn't believe what he read. Five cruisers and five destroyers! They can't be that close! thought the officer.

Then suddenly, with no break in the madness of battle, there was more trouble.

Crew loads bombs on a plane at Midway.

A screaming, roaring noise caused the Japanese to look upward in fear. Up there somewhere fifteen American Flying Fortresses (B-17s) were dropping bombs—from 20,000 feet. They were too high to be shot down!

The Japanese ships sloshed and bobbed through the water. They waited to be blown to bits. But not one single bomb hit its target.

Relieved that the gods had smiled on them, the Japanese high command called back all their planes.

"Bring them home!" came the order. "They are low on fuel! Bring all of them back to the decks!"

The planes swarmed back toward the carriers. The Japanese fleet continued to chug forward on a steady course. The Japanese fleet was heading straight toward the American fleet.

The Japanese aircraft appeared through the clouds and screeched and glided to a halt on the decks. The crews clambered over them, working furiously. They readied thirty-eight dive-bombers, fifty-four torpedo-bombers, and all the fighting escorts.

Crew members began to talk among themselves. This was it, they knew. For a long time there had been talk about the "Decisive Battle of the Pacific." Now this was about to take place.

"Hurry!" shouted one member of the Japanese crew. "When this is all over we will control these entire waters!"

This same optimism was shared by the Japanese commanders.

They, too, felt confident that victory was near at hand. After all, the American bombing attacks had been pitifully inaccurate. If that was any example of the American's fighting ability, the United States fleet should be no problem. When the American fleet was out of the way, the Japanese troops could land on Midway and take the islands.

The Japanese did not realize, however, that the Americans were not quivering back in fear. The United States figured out that the enemy had recalled the planes for one reason—to refuel and to reload bombs and torpedoes.

"If we could just hit them now!" said an American. "If we could just let them have it while they're refueling their planes!"

"We could move up the attack," his companion said. "The trouble is—it's risky. Once the fighting starts our planes have barely enough fuel to return."

"It's a shame to let them just sit there refueling, when we could move in and take them out."

An Avenger torpedo plane takes off from the deck of an aircraft carrier.

Rear Admiral Spruance felt the same way. He moved up the attack. Every operational plane in the area was ordered into the fracas. A total of sixty-seven dive-bombers, twenty fighters, and twenty-nine torpedo planes were soon off the ships and into the sky.

A few hours later, even more planes were ordered to leave the decks. This time another seventeen dive-bombers took off, along with six fighters and twelve torpedo planes.

But the Japanese fleet wanted to get itself out of the hot seat created by the Americans. The ships veered sharply and changed directions. It was an evasive action. Because of it, the American planes couldn't find the Japanese ships. It was as if the entire enemy fleet had disappeared from the Pacific. There was nothing below but blue ocean.

"Something better pop soon," came an American pilot's voice, "or I'll be flying off fumes. Our fuel is low."

"Just destroy the ships," came a reply.

"Yes sir," said the pilot sarcastically, "as soon as I find them." One group leader, however, didn't follow the rest. He had a hunch the enemy had gone in a different direction. He couldn't say why exactly. His name was John Waldron. He was part Sioux Indian. He led his squadron in a different direction.

His hunch was right. Soon, far below, he spotted the mighty Japanese carriers. They were steaming along in a formation that looked like a box.

Suddenly—with no warning—about thirty Zeros swarmed up to attack the American planes.

Lieutenant Commander John Waldron (left) and his squadron of fifteen TBD Devastator torpedo-bombers were the first to locate the Japanese fleet. Before they could attack, however, they were intercepted by nearly fifty Zeros. All fifteen American planes were shot down.

They seemed to be everywhere. But Waldron calmly paid them no attention. He wanted the ships. And he was determined to sink as many as he could.

Gunfire ripped above the roar of the engines. Two United States Devastators screamed downward into the ocean. Still Waldron led his men toward the fleet. As the American planes came down closer, anti-aircraft guns whacked out another Devastator.

Suddenly Waldron's plane was hit. He stood up, struggling to bail out of the cockpit. He never made it. His plane screamed downward out of control and crashed, killing him and his companion.

Only one Devastator was left now, and the pilot bored in. The noise of the battle, however, had pinpointed the Japanese fleet for the other American planes. As the single Devastator zoomed downward to take on the enemy single-handedly, it was suddenly joined by other American aircraft.

"Thought you could use a little help," crackled a pilot's voice over the radio. Together they made a giant, howling sweep at the Japanese ships.

When they swept back up into the clouds they saw that not one Japanese ship was going down.

"Holy cow, you guys!" some pilot wisecracked. "You couldn't hit a bull in the behind with a bass fiddle!"

Discouraged almost beyond belief, the Americans kept fighting. They were more determined than ever. The group of planes was joined by still more Americans. The air above and the water below were a howling roar of confusion, gunfire, and death.

Then the Americans scored a hit! The *Kaga* was blasted into flames, hit in the forward, aft, and middle decks.

"Let's see you beat that, wise guy," an American pilot said. "What was that about a bull and a bass fiddle?"

Then, a second hit! The *Akagi* suddenly lurched. The planes on its deck exploded. The bombs and the torpedoes and the boxes of ammunition aboard the ship went up in a wild swoosh of deadly fire.

Then the third Japanese carrier—the *Soryu*—felt the angry whap of American bullets and bombs and torpedoes. Within fifty-four minutes the American planes wiped out three Japanese carriers.

Only the incredibly lucky *Hiryu* was left. The Japanese commander aboard *Hiryu* ordered planes into the air. The Japanese pilots took off after the *Yorktown*.

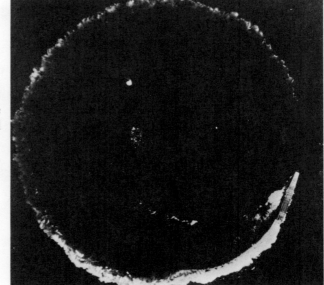

The Japanese carrier *Soryu* made a complete circle to try to avoid American bombs. She was hit, however, and sank a few hours later.

"Attack!" came the command.

The Japanese planes roared down on the American ship. Two boilers aboard the *Yorktown* exploded. She was crippled badly.

But the Americans had the raging fire under control within half an hour and the *Yorktown* limped on its way.

"Get that ship!" shouted a Japanese, seeing what had happened.

Once more planes took off from the *Hiryu* deck. They came down on *Yorktown* and, this time, scored with two torpedoes. Finally, at 3 P.M., the *Yorktown*—dead in the water—was abandoned.

While the Japanese were attacking *Yorktown*, the American fleet was launching more and more planes to chase down the enemy. They swarmed like bees, fighting their way through the anti-aircraft barrage. They zapped down on the *Hiryu*. The lucky Japanese ship suddenly ran out of luck. It burst into a fiery swoosh of flame and smoke.

"That should do it!" an American pilot said. "Let's get out of here!"

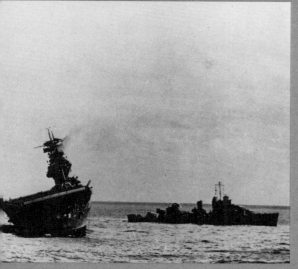

The crew of the United States carrier *Yorktown* (top left) tries to put out fires caused by Japanese bombs and torpedoes. The ship was too badly damaged to be repaired, however, and was abandoned (top right). The following day, as the *Yorktown* was being towed back to Pearl Harbor (bottom left), she was sunk by two torpedoes from the Japanese submarine I-168 (bottom right).

Seeing that all four Japanese carriers were hit, the Americans pulled back.

Although hurt badly, the Japanese still wanted to fight. There was one last chance. They would try to lure the American fleet into a surface fight. If this could be done, the Japanese believed they could still defeat the Americans and win the battle.

Deliberately, as a hunter stalks its game, the Japanese fleet began to track the Americans, trying to draw them into a surface fight.

But the United States would have no part of it. The American fleet gracefully backed off. And waited.

At 7:13 P.M. there was a terrible explosion aboard the wounded *Soryu*. The powerful carrier pitched and began to sink. It hissed like a giant snake as the fire met the water and the carrier slipped under. With her, 718 men went down. Some of them were dead, others were trapped inside. Only one man—Captain Yanagimoto—died deliberately aboard the *Soryu*. He tied himself to the bridge and went down with his ship, refusing to abandon her.

The Japanese heavy cruiser *Mikuma* was only wreckage after a collision with a sister ship and an attack by American planes.

The Americans waited.

Then, forty miles south of the spot where *Soryu* hissed into her grave, the *Kaga* burned out of control. In only a short time there were two huge explosions that ripped through the early morning. The *Kaga*, with eight hundred men aboard, went down forever.

The Americans waited. They still refused to be baited into a surface fight. The Japanese leaders realized they could do nothing now but turn back and try to make it home.

The once mighty Japanese fleet wobbled away
with what was left—the *Hiryu* and the *Akagi*. Both
ships were burned black by the rampaging fires
caused by the American attack.

Afraid the ships would be captured by the
Americans—and for some strange reason placed
in a museum in San Francisco—the Japanese
torpedoed *Akagi* and sent her to the bottom of the
sea. The following afternoon, the Japanese
deliberately sank the *Hiryu*.

It was all over. One of the most important
battles of World War II had been fought. When
the smoke and the fire and the destruction ended,
the Americans had won the Battle of Midway.

The United States controlled the Pacific and
Japan had started its descent into total defeat.

The Japanese carrier *Akagi* (below) was damaged by an American air attack and then
was torpedoed and sunk by the Japanese.

About the Author

A native of Alabama, G.C. Skipper has traveled throughout the
world, including Jamaica, Haiti, India, Argentina, the Bahamas,
and Mexico. He has written several other children's books as well as
an adult novel. Mr. Skipper has also published numerous articles in
national magazines. He is now working on his second adult novel.
Mr. Skipper and his family live in Norristown, Pennsylvania, a
suburb of Philadelphia.